sous vide

Gourmet

edited by Mary Dan Eades

photography by Mehosh Dziadzio

Paradox Press

contents

introduction

Though elite chefs in multi-star restaurants have relied on the sous vide technique to cook fabulous food for decades—it's what enables them to reliably produce exquisite dishes time after time for scores of diners—the trend to move this "culinary secret" out of the restaurant kitchen and onto the kitchen countertop is a fairly recent phenomenon. In a short space of time—only a couple of years, really—foodies and DIY gourmet cooks have eagerly embraced sous vide cooking as a means to create such perfection themselves at home. All they've lacked so far are cookbooks to guide them. There are good collections of recipes for doing simple basic sous vide cooking, and good (expensive) coffee-table-quality books for elite restaurant chefs and molecular gastronomists. But for the excellent home cook, who yearns to experiment with exotic ingredients, delights in beautiful plating, revels in bringing out the best in whatever is being cooked, and thus wants to embrace sous vide, there's been little guidance.

This book will help to fill that void. In it, an all-star lineup of America's culinary greats offers up some of their favorite sous vide creations, pairing complex flavors and interesting ingredients in a format doable by the home chef, along with complete plating instructions and side dish pairings. With step-by-step instructions to guide you, you'll soon be cooking like the pros at home, creating mouthwatering, gourmet, sous vide dishes that will wow your family and friends. But before you get started on gourmet sous vide cooking, let us introduce your teachers.

Alex Seidel, Chef and Owner of **Fruition Restaurant**, Denver, Colorado
The James Beard Foundation has recognized Chef Seidel with several nominations for "Best Chef Southwest" and also with an invitation to cook for the 20th Anniversary "Dinners across America." *Food and Wine* magazine named him as one of its 2010 "Best New Chefs in America."

Phillip Foss, Chef and Blogger for the**pickeledtongue**.com, Chicago, Illinois
Chef Foss was the Executive Chef at Lockwood Restaurant in Chicago when it was awarded three stars by the *Chicago Tribune* and the *Chicago Sun-Times*, four diamonds by AAA, and named as one of the *Chicago Tribune's* "Top 10 Best New Restaurants." *Chicago Social* also named him first runner-up as the "Best New Chef" in town.

Jason Wilson, Chef and Owner, **CRUSH**, Seattle, Washington
In 2006, Chef Wilson was declared one of the "Top Ten New Chefs in North America" by the prestigious *Food and Wine* magazine, and in 2010 was awarded "Best Chef Northwest" by the James Beard Foundation.

Michael Solomonov, Chef and Owner of **Zahav** in Philadelphia, Pennsylvania
James Beard Foundation Winner "Best Chef Mid-Atlantic 2011," Chef Solomonov not only dishes up Israeli cuisine at Zahav, but has gone global with Xochitl, a Mexican eatery, and down-home with Percy Street Barbecue, both also in Philadelphia. In February 2011, he wowed television's "Iron Chef" judges with his passion fruit infused malabi custard dessert.

~ Mary Dan Eades, Editor

the basics

Cooking sous vide (a French term meaning *under vacuum*) involves vacuum-sealing a given food—meat, fish, poultry, vegetables, fruit—in a food-grade cooking pouch and submerging it in a temperature-controlled water bath for as long as it takes to bring the food to the desired temperature throughout. Food cooks gently and precisely and cannot overcook, since it can only reach the temperature of the water in the bath. Flavor and moisture that would normally escape into the air or drip into the pan stay locked in the food pouch, which produces the most flavorful, tender, and juicy food possible.

Chef George Pralus developed the technique in France about 40 years ago as a method for perfectly cooking and minimizing the costly shrinkage of foie gras. Chef Bruno Goussalt popularized the technique by introducing it in the first-class cabin cuisine on Air France's international flights. Since then, it has become a favored cooking technique of great chefs around the globe, and the secret weapon of chefs in competitions.

The introduction in 2009 of the SousVide Supreme,™ the first water oven designed for kitchen countertops, made the technique practical for everyone, from the rank novice to the accomplished cook.

How does sous vide cooking work?

Unlike traditional cooking methods, such as roasting, broiling, grilling, or sautéing, that use aggressively high temperatures to heat the air around the food, the sous vide technique relies on the superior ability of water to transfer heat to food. Because the transfer of heat through water is many times faster than the transfer of heat through air, removing all, or at least most, of the air from the cooking pouch—creating the vacuum seal—is important, as pockets of air between the pouch and the food can result in uneven cooking.

When cooking sous vide, the water bath temperature is set at precisely the desired target for doneness—for instance, 146°F (63.5°C) for perfectly done chicken breasts. Foods cook gently for (at a minimum) long enough to allow the heat of the water to penetrate to the center of the food. How long that process takes has been carefully worked out mathematically for a wide variety of food types, and depends not as much on the weight of the food being cooked as on its thickness. For example, if it takes 40 minutes to bring a piece of chicken that is one-inch thick to temperature, it might take two hours to bring a two-inch thick piece to that temperature. It is important, for food safety, to carefully adhere to the minimum cooking times and holding instructions.

The simple steps of sous vide cooking

1. Season your food lightly with salt and pepper, or fresh or dried herbs and spices.

2. Seal the food in an appropriately sized food-grade cooking pouch. There are several types of cooking pouches and sealing methods. A chamber vacuum sealer will seal both solids and liquids in cooking pouches, as well as in a variety of storage containers. A suction sealer may be used to seal pouches containing less than a tablespoon of liquid; and zip-seal cooking pouches provide a convenient and inexpensive way to seal liquid-rich foods. By simply lowering the filled, unsealed zip pouch into the water bath, the air is displaced by the water, and the zip-closure can be sealed when it reaches the surface.

3. Simmer the food at the desired temperature in the preheated water bath for at least the minimum recommended amount of time to ensure it is heated to the center. In most cases, you can leave the food in the water bath substantially longer without loss of quality.

4. Sear or sauce your food, if desired. All foods that have been cooked sous vide will

be delicious straight from the pouch; but some benefit from a complementary sauce or a quick sear in a hot skillet, on a grill, or with a kitchen torch to impart the expected crisp, golden crust.

Tips for sous vide cooking

Plan your menu in advance. Cook foods that need some time (spare ribs, short ribs, flank steak, pork roast, pork belly, and tough or grass fed cuts) over night or even a couple of days. Quick-chill them thoroughly (see page 11) and refrigerate. Then cook foods that take the shortest amount of time.

Group foods together according to the temperatures that they cook. Red meats (beef, lamb) can all cook at the same temperature to your preferred degree of done-ness: rare, medium-rare, medium, medium-well. White meats (chicken or turkey breast) and pork (chops, ribs, or roasts) can cook at the same temperature. Chicken, turkey or duck thighs and legs cook hotter—176°F (80°C)—and longer, so they're a breeze to do overnight. Fruits and vegetables of every type can cook at the same temperature—in the range of 180°F (82°C) to 185°F (85°C)—in about 30 minutes to an hour-and-a-half, depending on their size and tenderness or toughness.

The length of cooking required depends on two things: thickness of the food in the pouch and its tenderness or toughness. Tender cuts merely need to be brought to the desired temperature—perhaps 45 minutes to an hour for a 1-inch piece of steak— then finished with a quick sear. Though they may be heated through in the same hour, long, slow cooking of short ribs (48 hours) or lamb belly (36 hours) allows their plentiful collagen to gelatinize and melt, giving them succulence and transforming their tough-ness into pull-apart tenderness.

Food safety in sous vide cooking

As with all cooking methods, it is important to use clean, fresh ingredients and to work with clean hands and tools on clean surfaces. When cooking food sous vide for immediate consumption—what is termed Cook-Serve—the basic rules of food handling will suffice, because the food will remain hot in the machine until serving and will get a final high-temperature sear.

Sometimes, especially when entertaining, it is helpful to employ a technique, used widely by restaurant chefs, called Cook-Chill-Hold. In this method, food is vacuum-sealed and cooked to completion in the water oven in advance, and then quick-chilled in an ice water bath for long enough to return it to refrigerator temperature, and out of the so-called "danger zone." The danger zone is the temperature range between 40°F (5°C) and 130°F (54°C) where food-borne bacteria can grow most easily. Even though most of the potentially harmful bacteria will be killed by sous vide cooking, some can protect themselves from the heat by hibernating as dormant forms—called spores—that can blossom again given sufficient time and favorable temperatures.

To reduce the risk of food-borne illness when using the Cook-Chill-Hold method, follow these important guidelines:

• Quick-chill the warm cooking pouches of food fully submerged in an ice water bath (half ice and half water) for long enough to ensure a quick drop back to refrigerated temperature. Generally this will be the same length as the minimum time required to bring the food to temperature. Add ice or freezer packs as needed.

• Immediately after chilling either refrigerate or freeze in the pouch.

• Hold refrigerated pouches of sous vide cooked food for no more than 48 hours; properly frozen food pouches should remain safe for up to one year.

• To ensure safety in holding, particularly with home refrigerators, be sure the refrigerator compartment maintains a temperature below 40°F (5°C), and that the freezer maintains a temperature below 0°F (-17°C).

Alex
Seidel

Chef and Owner of Fruition Restaurant in Denver, Colorado

15

warm artichoke salad

17

grissini bread sticks

19

artichoke dip

21

black olive crusted petrale sole

23

fennel and pepper stew

24

potato brandade gnocchi

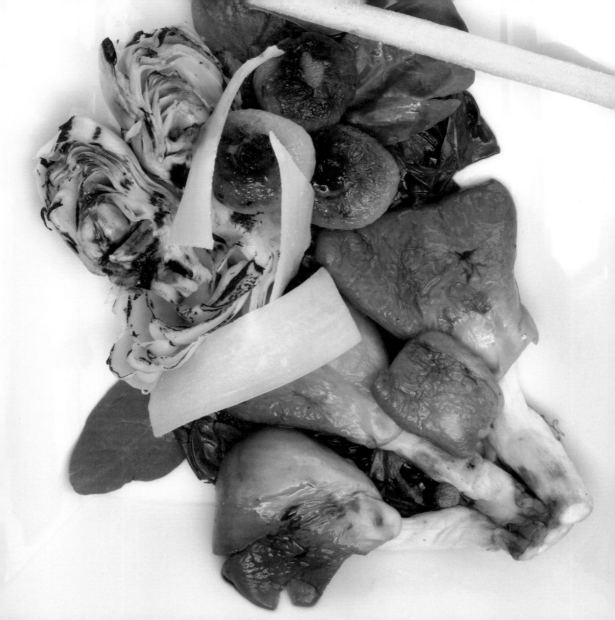

salad

Serves 4
Cooking time: 1½ hours

1. Fill and preheat the water oven to 185°F (85°C).

2. Fill a bowl, large enough to hold the artichokes, with water and add the juice of the two lemons.

3. Clean the artichokes using a vegetable peeler and cut them in half; immediately drop the halves into the acidulated (lemon) water to keep them from oxidizing.

1 quart (32 fl oz/0.9 liters) water

2 lemons

36 fresh baby artichokes

2 cups (16 fl oz/473 ml) vegetable stock

2 tablespoons (15 ml) olive oil

Salt, to taste

12 cipollini onions

For plating

4 cups (4.2 oz/120 g) fresh spinach

12 reserved baby artichoke halves

1 cup (2.5 oz/70 g) oyster mushrooms

12 reserved cipollini onions

Artichoke Dip (page 19)

Aged balsamic vinegar, for garnish

Parmigiano-Reggiano, shaved, for garnish

Grissini Bread Sticks (page 17)

4. Remove the artichokes from the water and put them in a single, even layer into a large (1 gallon/3.8 liter) chamber vacuum pouch or zip-closure cooking pouch. Add the vegetable stock, a drizzle of olive oil and sprinkle of salt, and vacuum seal the chamber vacuum pouch, or use Archimedes' Principle (page 60) and seal the zip pouch.

5. Submerge the pouch and cook for 1 hour and 30 minutes.

6. Quick chill, submerged in an ice water bath (half ice, half water) for 15 to 20 minutes. Open the pouch, remove 12 halves to reserve for plating. The remainder will be used for the Artichoke Dip (page 17).

7. Meanwhile, caramelize the cipollini onions in a large sauté pan over medium heat with a bit of olive oil until they are golden all over. Set aside.

Chef's recommended plating

1. Grill the fresh spinach and the 12 reserved artichoke halves on an oiled grill or grill pan to warm and mark them.

2. In a skillet, sauté the oyster mushrooms and warm the cipollini onions.

3. Warm the artichoke dip on the stovetop, or keep warm in a cooking pouch in the water oven set at 160°F (71°C).

4. On one end of a rectangular plate, mound artichoke dip in a ring mold, press gently and remove ring.

5. Pile grilled spinach down the length of the plate.

6. Arrange the mushrooms, onions, and grilled artichokes on top of the spinach.

7. Garnish with drops of aged balsamic and curls of shaved Parmigianino-Reggiano.

8. Place 2 or 3 bread sticks diagonally across the plate.

grissini
bread sticks

½ tablespoon (7.5 ml) dry active yeast

¼ cup (2 fl oz/60 ml) water at body temperature: 98°F (37°C)

1½ tablespoon (22.5 ml) sugar

½ cup (4 fl oz/120 ml) milk

2 cups (9.6 oz/272 g) bread flour

1½ tablespoons (22.5 ml) olive oil

Makes 4 dozen
Cooking time: 15 to 30 minutes

1. Preheat the traditional oven to 350°F (176.5°C).

2. In a small mixing bowl combine the yeast, water, and sugar and proof for 4 or 5 minutes (bubbles will begin to form as the yeast begins to work.)

3. After the yeast mixture has proofed, add it to the bowl of an electric mixer, add the milk, and mix on low speed to incorporate.

4. Add the flour and olive oil and knead at low speed until it makes a well-formed ball that pulls away from the sides of the bowl.

5. Cover the bowl and move it to a warm place in the kitchen to let the dough rise.

6. When the dough has doubled in size, punch down.

7. Roll the dough flat, using either a pasta roller or a rolling pin, to a ¼-inch (0.6 cm) thickness.

8. Cut the dough into strips ¼-inch (0.6 cm) wide and 6-inches (9.5 cm) long.

9. Roll each strip by hand to form into a round stick.

10. Put the sticks on a parchment-lined baking sheet and bake until crispy and slightly golden brown—about 15 minutes.

artichoke
dip

Serves 4
Preparation time: 20 minutes

2 cups (16 fl oz/473 ml) heavy cream

60 baby artichoke halves cooked sous vide (page 15)

½ cup (3 oz/90 g) grated Parmigiano-Reggiano (or other Parmesan cheese)

Salt and white pepper to taste

3 cups (3.2 oz/90 g) spinach, blanched and drained well

½ cup (4 oz/113 g) cream cheese

2 tablespoons (30 ml) fresh oregano leaves

1. In a heavy saucepan, reduce the cream by half.

2. Add half the baby artichokes and Parmesan and season with salt and white pepper.

3. Rough chop the other half of the artichokes and reserve.

4. Rough chop half the spinach and reserve.

5. In a food service blender or food processor, put the artichoke cream mixture, remaining spinach, cream cheese and oregano, and blend until smooth

6. Push the mixture through a fine mesh strainer and cool.

7. When the mixture has cooled, fold in the reserved chopped artichokes and spinach.

black olive crusted
petrale sole

Serves 4
Cooking time: 15 minutes

1. Fill and preheat the water oven to 143°F (61.5°C), and preheat the traditional oven to 400°F (204°C.)

2. In a bowl, prepare the crust by mixing the olives, breadcrumbs, pine nuts, and parsley; season with salt and pepper to taste. Set aside.

3. Season the filets with a bit of salt and pepper.

4. Tear 4 sheets of plastic wrap about 12 inches long and have ready.

5. Working with one filet at a time, roulade (roll) each portion of fish along its length and wrap tightly in the plastic wrap to hold the shape.

12 to 14 (2.8 oz/84g) sun-dried black olives, roughly chopped

¼ cup (0.5 oz/14 g) panko breadcrumbs

¼ cup (1 oz/30 g) pine nuts, roughly chopped

1 teaspoon (5 ml) parsley, chopped

Salt and white pepper, to taste

4 (5½ oz/163 g) portions petrale sole

¼ cup (2 fl oz/60 ml) grapeseed oil

4 egg whites (reserve yolks for gnocchi on page 24, if making)

For the beurre fondue

1 cup (8 fl oz/240 ml) dry white wine

1 tablespoon (15 ml) white wine vinegar

1 sprig thyme

6 white peppercorns

2 small shallots, peeled and sliced

½ cup (4 fl oz/120 ml) heavy cream

1 stick (4 oz/113 g) unsalted butter

1 teaspoon (5 ml) lemon zest

2 tablespoons (30 ml) capers, rinsed and drained

Salt and white pepper, to taste

For plating

Fennel and Pepper Stew (page 22)

Potato Brandade Gnocchi (page 23)

Fennel fronds, for garnish

6. Put the fish roulades into a small (1 quart/0.9 liter) cooking pouch and vacuum seal.

7. Submerge the pouch in the water bath to cook for 8 minutes and remove. If not finishing right away, quick chill the pouch submerged in ice water (half ice, half water) for 5 minutes and refrigerate for up to 24 hours.

8. To finish, remove the fish from the pouch, and remove and discard the plastic wrap.

9. Heat the oil in large sauté pan and sear the rolls until golden brown, presentation side down.

10. Flip them over, brush the presentation side with egg white and sprinkle liberally with the breadcrumb mixture.

11. Transfer the pan to the traditional oven and bake for 4 to 5 minutes, or until the crust is golden brown.

12. Meanwhile, make the beurre fondue in a small sauce pot by combining the wine, vinegar, thyme, peppercorns and shallots.

13. Simmer to *au sec* (nearly dry), add the cream, bring back to a simmer, and allow the sauce to reduce to a thick and sticky consistency.

14. Slowly whisk butter into the mixture, a few cubes at a time, allowing it to melt before adding more.

15. Season with the lemon zest and capers and salt and pepper to taste.

16. Reserve warm.

Chef's recommended plating

1. Spoon a fourth of the Fennel and Pepper Stew into a large entrée bowl.

2. Coat the Potato Brandade Gnocchi in the beurre fondue and then spoon a few around the stew on each plate.

3. Place one filet in each dish on top of the stew and garnish with fennel fronds.

fennel
and pepper
stew

Serves 4
Cooking time: 30 minutes

1. In a large pot over low heat, warm the oil; add the fennel, peppers, onions and garlic and sweat until tender.

2. Add the tomato juice, bring to boil, then turn down to simmer for 30 minutes.

3. Season with salt, pepper, parsley, red chile flakes and red wine vinegar.

4. Reserve warm.

2 tablespoons (30 ml) grapeseed oil

1 bulb fennel, stalks removed, sliced julienne, fronds reserved for garnish

1 red bell pepper, stemmed, seeded, and sliced julienne

1 yellow bell pepper, stemmed, seeded, and sliced julienne

1 red onion, peeled and sliced julienne

1 yellow onion, peeled and sliced julienne

2 cloves garlic, peeled and thinly sliced

16 ounces (473 g) San Marzano tomatoes, for juice only (squeeze juice out of whole tomatoes, reserve tomatoes for another use)

Salt and white pepper, to taste

1 teaspoon (5 ml) parsley

1/8 teaspoon (0.6 ml) red chile pepper flakes

1 tablespoon (15 ml) red wine vinegar

potato brandade

gnocchi

Serves 4
Cooking time: 1 hour

1. Fill and preheat the water oven to 180°F (82°C).

2. Put the potatoes into large (1 gallon/3.8 liter) cooking pouches and vacuum seal.

1 pound Yukon gold potatoes, peeled and diced to 1 inch (2.5 cm)

4 ounces (120 g) salt cod, soaked for two days in water

4 cloves garlic, peeled and blanched in milk to cover 3 times

1 cup (8 fl oz/240 ml) whole milk

1½ to 2 cups (6.75-9 oz/199-266 g) all-purpose flour

4 egg yolks

3 tablespoons (45 ml) olive oil

Salt and white pepper, to taste

2 tablespoons (30 ml) grapeseed oil

2 tablespoons (30 ml) butter

1½ to 2 cups (12 to 16 fl oz/ 355 to 473 ml) water

3. Submerge the pouches in the water bath to cook for 30 to 45 minutes, until tender when pressed through the pouch.

4. Meanwhile, rinse the salt cod under cold water.

5. In a saucepan over low heat, combine the cod, blanched garlic, milk, and enough water to cover; bring to a simmer and cook for 15 minutes.

6. Strain off the liquid, reserving the solids for step 7.

7. In a stand mixer, fitted with a paddle attachment, process the fish mixture on slow to medium speed until the fish is broken to rice-sized flakes. Reserve warm.

8. Open the potato pouches, drain off the liquid, and run the potatoes through a food mill.

9. Put the potatoes into a large mixing bowl, sprinkle the cod mixture over them, and then add flour, eggs and olive oil, and season with salt and pepper.

10. Gently work the mixture with a wooden spoon until the dough just begins to come together.

11. Pour the mixture out onto a flat surface and divide into quarters.

12. Roll out each quarter into a long snake-shaped roll, dusting often with flour to avoid sticking, and cut the rolls into 1-inch (2.5-cm) pillows.

13. Put the gnocchi pillows in a single layer into large (1 gallon/3.8 liter) cooking pouches and seal only; do not vacuum or you will crush them. Store in the freezer for as long as 2 to 3 days.

14. Before plating, sear the gnocchi from frozen in a sauté pan over medium heat in grapeseed oil until golden on both sides.

15. Add the butter and enough water to cover the gnocchi. Continue to cook until the gnocchi rise to the surface of the water, about 1 minute more.

16. Strain off the liquid, and reserve the gnocchi in a bowl.

Phillip
Foss

Chef and Blogger, thepickeledtongue.com, Chicago, Illinois

29

Scottish wood pigeon

31

pickeled foraged mushrooms and ramps

32

sassafras and ginger pudding

33

fig-mint of lamb

36

braised leeks

37

pea soup

Scottish
wood pigeon

2 Scottish wood pigeons

2 tablespoons (30 ml) olive oil

Salt and pepper

2 sassafras branches or 12-inch (30 cm) wooden skewers

For plating

Assortment of foraged greens (wood sorrel, purslane, mallow, amaranth, sweet clover, lamb's quarter) or watercress leaves

Pickled Foraged Mushrooms and Ramps (page 31)

Sassafras and Ginger Pudding (page 32)

3 cactus fruit, peeled and quartered

Serves 2
Cooking time: 35 minutes

1. Fill and preheat the water oven to 139°F (59.5°C).

2. Remove the breasts and legs from the wood pigeons, separate the legs from the thighs, and bone the thighs.

3. Cut the breasts and thighs in half, put all pieces into a bowl, and toss them in the olive oil, salt, and pepper.

4. Arrange the pieces in an even single layer in a cooking pouch and vacuum seal.

5. Submerge the pouch in the water bath and cook for 20 to 30 minutes.

6. Meanwhile, soak the branches or skewers in water for 20 minutes, and preheat a grill to high heat.

7. Open the pouch and skewer the pigeon pieces on the sassafras branches or wooden skewers.

8. Sear the meat quickly on all sides on the grill. Remove the skewered pigeon to a wire rack to rest, and keep warm under a tent of foil.

Chef's recommended plating

1. In a bowl of ice water, shock the fresh foraged greens and drain on a paper towel.

2. Remove the Pickled Foraged Mushrooms and Ramps from their liquid and drain on a paper towel.

3. Squeeze or spoon the Sassafras and Ginger Pudding down the middle of each plate and place a wood pigeon skewer on top of the pudding.

4. Arrange the pickled mushrooms, ramps, greens, and cactus fruit pieces around each skewer.

mushrooms

2 cups (5 oz/140 g) assorted wild mushrooms (wild enoki, lion's mane, maitake, oyster, pheasant back, golden pholeota, puff balls, bluettes, honey mushrooms, entoloma)

4 wild ramp bulbs

1 cup (8 fl oz/240 ml) water

½ cup (4 fl oz/120 ml) white wine vinegar

1 tablespoon (15 ml) sugar

1 sprig sage

1 teaspoon (5 ml) salt

Serves 4
Cooking time: 15 minutes

1. Clean the mushrooms and ramps and put them into a large (1 gallon/3.8 liter) chamber vacuum pouch or zip-closure cooking pouch and set aside.

2. In a pot over high heat, combine the remaining ingredients and bring to a boil.

3. Pour the pickling liquid over the mushrooms and ramps and vacuum seal in the chamber vacuum, or use Archimedes' Principle (page 60) to remove the air from the zip pouch and seal.

4. Quick chill the pouch, completely submerged in an ice water bath (half ice, half water) for 30 minutes and store in the refrigerator for up to 48 hours.

5. Serve chilled.

sassafras  and ginger pudding

1½ cups (12 fl oz/355 ml) water

2 ounces (55 g) sassafras

1 teaspoon (5 g) wild ginger

2 tablespoons (30 ml) ULTRA-TEX® 8

ULTRA-TEX® 8 is a modified food starch derived from tapioca. It provides high viscosity and a smooth, rich and creamy texture. It's available through restaurant suppliers and many online vendors, including amazon.com.

Serves 2
Cooking time: 1 hour

1. Put the water, sassafras and ginger In a pot over high heat.

2. Bring to a boil and allow the liquid to infuse for 1 hour.

3. Strain through a chinois, and pour into a blender. With the motor running, add the ULTRA-TEX slowly and process to emulsify the mixture to a pudding consistency.

fig-mint

of lamb

8 ounces (226 g) dried figs

¼ bunch fresh mint

¼ bunch Italian parsley

2½ cups (20 fl oz/591 ml) water

2 tablespoons (30 ml) balsamic vinegar

2 tablespoons (30 ml) brown sugar

1½ tablespoons (22.5 ml) freshly ground black pepper

1 rack of lamb, tenderloin removed from the bone (or left on the rack, if desired, and sliced into portions at plating)

Salt and pepper, to taste

For plating

Braised Leeks (page 36)

Pea Soup (page 37)

Serves 4
Cooking time: 1 hour

1. Trim the stems from the figs, mint and parsley.

2. In a blender or food processor, purée the figs, herbs, half the water, the vinegar, brown sugar and black pepper.

3. Add the rest of the water and continue to process a minute or so more.

4. Taste the marinade. It should have notes of sweetness, acidity from the vinegar and a good dose of spice from the black pepper. Adjust the seasoning to your liking.

5. Put the lamb into a small (1 quart/0.9 liter) chamber vacuum pouch or zip-closure cooking pouch, cover with the marinade, and vacuum seal in the chamber vacuum, or use Archimedes' Principle to remove the air from the zip pouch and seal.

6. Marinate overnight in the refrigerator.

7. Fill and preheat the water oven to 134°F (56.5°C) for medium-rare lamb.

8. Submerge the pouch in the water bath and cook for 1 hour.

9. When ready to finish, preheat an oiled charcoal grill or grill pan to high heat.

10. Remove the lamb from the pouch and wipe off excess marinade.

11. Cut the lamb tenderloin into four uniform pieces. Season lightly with salt and fresh cracked black pepper, if needed.

12. Sear the lamb quickly on all sides, and transfer to a wire rack to rest for 1 to 2 minutes before serving.

Chef's recommended plating

1. Spoon the Braised Leeks into the center of four warm bowls and position the lamb portions on top.

2. Pour the hot Pea Soup around the lamb and serve.

leaks

8 cups (25 oz/712 g) leeks,
diced large

½ cup (4 fl oz/120 ml) extra virgin
olive oil

Salt, to taste

Serves 4
Cooking time: 15 minutes

1. Thoroughly wash the diced leeks, rinse well to remove all grit, and dry them.

2. Heat the olive oil over medium heat in a non-reactive, heavy-gauge sauce pan large enough to comfortably fit the leeks without overcrowding and without excessive spacing.

3. Add the leeks, season with salt, and cook until the water has cooked out.

4. If not serving immediately, spread the leeks out over as much surface as possible to cool to room temperature.

pea
soup

4 cups (20.5 oz/580 g) shucked, fresh peas (substitute with frozen)

1½ cups (12 fl oz/340 ml) chicken stock

Salt, to taste

Serves 4
Cooking time: 10 minutes

1. Bring a large pot of salted water to a boil and blanch the peas until tender (about 3 minutes).

2. Transfer to an ice bath, cool completely, and drain. (If using frozen peas, thaw completely before continuing.)

3. Put the peas in a blender and add the cold chicken stock. Blend over high speed until very smooth (about 3 minutes).

4. Season to taste, and bring to a boil just before serving.

Jason
Wilson

Chef and Owner of CRUSH in Seattle, Washington

41

sassafras scented duck breast

42

soubise sauce

43

sous vide octopus

46

pickled green tomatoes

47

white corn pudding

48

herb roasted lamb loin

sassafras scented
duck breast

2 tablespoons (30 ml) sassafras powder

1 1/2 tablespoons (45 ml) kosher salt

4 sprigs fresh thyme, stripped for leaves

1/2 teaspoon (2.5 ml) ground black cardamom

4 Moulard duck breasts, trimmed of silver skin and excess fat

For plating

Soubise Sauce (page 42)

1/2 cup (2.4 oz/68 g) huckleberries

8 figs

Serves 4
Cooking time: 45 minutes

1. Fill and preheat the water oven to 140°F (60°C).

2. In a small bowl, combine the seasonings and spices, mixing well.

3. Season the duck with the spice mixture. Put 2 breasts in a single layer in each of 2 small (1 quart/0.9 liter) cooking pouches and vacuum seal.

4. Submerge the pouches in the water bath and cook for 20 to 30 minutes.

5. Remove the breasts from the pouches and allow 5 minutes for the meat to rest.

6. In a sauté pan over medium heat, slowly sear the breasts, fat side down, until fat is rendered and skin is crisp.

Chef's recommended plating

1. Spoon a fourth of the Soubise Sauce onto each serving plate.

2. Place a duck breast on top of the sauce.

3. Garnish with huckleberries and figs.

soubise
sauce

Serves 4
Cooking time: 2¼ hours

1. Fill and preheat the water oven to 180°F (82°C).

2. Put all ingredients into a small (1 quart/0.9 liter) chamber vacuum pouch and vacuum seal, or into a small zip-closure cooking pouch, use Archimedes' Principle (page 60) to remove the air, and seal.

3. Submerge the pouch in the water bath and cook for 2 hours. (If not serving right away, quick chill the pouch by submerging it in an ice water bath—half ice, half water—for 30 minutes, and refrigerate up to 48 hours.)

4. When ready to use, pour the contents of the pouch into a blender, and puree until smooth.

5. Slowly simmer in a pot to warm for service.

1 yellow onion, peeled and rough chopped

1 shallot, peeled and rough chopped

1 strip bacon, diced small

½ green apple, peeled and acidulated

½ cup (4 fl oz/120 ml) heavy cream

1 bay leaf

1 stalk celery, trimmed and rough chopped

1 whole clove

2 sprigs thyme

2 tablespoons (30 ml) kosher salt

sousvide
octopus

Serves 6
Cooking time: 8½ hours

1. Fill and preheat the water oven to 156°F (69°C).

2. Thoroughly wash the octopi, and if using tentacles, cut them into bite-size pieces. Put them into a large bowl and set aside.

3. In a saucepan, over medium-high heat, make a marinade by combining all remaining ingredients, and simmer for 5 minutes.

30 baby octopi or 6 octopus tentacles, 4 to 5 inches (10 to 12 cm) each

¼ cup (2 fl oz/60 ml) olive oil

6 cloves garlic, peeled and smashed

1 tablespoon (15 ml) fresh orange zest

1 tablespoon (15 ml) kosher salt

1 teaspoon (5 ml) ground cumin

1 teaspoon (5 ml) pimenton (ground Spanish paprika)

1 teaspoon (5 ml) ground coriander

1 teaspoon (5 ml) chile flakes

6 stems Italian flat leaf parsley

For plating

Pickled Green Tomatoes (page 46)

White Corn Pudding (page 47)

4. Puree the marinade until smooth and pour it over the octopus, tossing to coat.

5. Arrange the octopi or tentacle pieces in a single, even layer in one or two large (1 gallon/3.8 liter) cooking pouches, fold over the end of the pouch, and secure with a clip.

6. Chill the pouch for 30 minutes in the freezer to firm the marinade for sealing.

7. Vacuum seal the pouches, submerge them in the water bath, and cook for 8 hours.

8. When ready to serve, remove the octopus from the pouches and quickly grill or sauté to finish.

Chef's recommended plating

1. On the serving plate, center a mound of the Pickled Green Tomatoes.

2. Arrange several octopi or the pieces of one tentacle atop the tomatoes.

3. Garnish the plate with a swoosh of the White Corn Pudding.

pickled green tomatoes

Serves 6
Cooking time: 5 minutes

4 cups (25 oz/720 g) green tomatoes, diced large

3 tablespoons (45 ml) kosher salt

2 tablespoons (30 ml) white sugar

1 teaspoon (5 ml) ground cumin

1 teaspoon (5 ml) coriander

1 tablespoon (15 ml) juniper berries

1 teaspoon (5 ml) fennel seeds

1 teaspoon (5 ml) cloves

1 teaspoon (5ml) chile flakes

6 cloves garlic, peeled and smashed

2 cups (16 fl oz/454 ml) cider vinegar

6 branches fresh mint

1. Put the tomatoes into a large non-reactive bowl or large (1 gallon/3.8 liter) zip-closure cooking pouch or chamber vacuum pouch.

2. In a saucepan over medium heat, mix together all remaining ingredients and simmer for 5 minutes to dissolve them and infuse their flavors.

3. Remove the mixture from the heat and allow 10 minutes for it to cool.

4. Pour the mixture through a strainer over the green tomatoes. Cover the bowl, or use Archimedes' Principle (page 60) and seal the zip pouch, or vacuum seal the chamber vacuum pouch.

5. Refrigerate and allow 24 hours for the tomatoes to pickle.

white corn
pudding

Serves 6
Cooking time: 30 minutes

½ cup (4 fl oz/120 ml) chicken stock

1 ounce (28 g) shallots, peeled and chopped

1½ teaspoons (7.5 ml) ground nutmeg

1½ teaspoons (7.5 ml) ground coriander

2 bay leaves

1½ teaspoons (7.5 ml) kosher salt, or to taste

32 ounces (907 g) white corn kernels

8 ounces (227 g) crème fraiche

4 stems fresh tarragon, stripped for leaves

2 to 4 stems lemon thyme, stripped for leaves

2 cups (16 fl oz/454 ml) fresh white corn juice

1. In a saucepan over medium heat, combine the chicken stock, shallots, nutmeg, coriander, bay leaves and salt, and simmer for 2 minutes.

2. Add the corn kernels and crème fraiche and continue to simmer for 10 minutes more, stirring constantly.

3. With a hand (immersion) blender, purée all ingredients well.

4. Add the fresh herbs and continue to purée until fairly smooth.

5. Add the corn juice and cook for 15 minutes over low heat, or until the mixture reaches a pudding consistency.

6. Adjust the seasoning and keep warm in a copper pot.
Alternately, keep warm in a water oven preheated to 140°F (60°C). To do so, transfer the pudding to a large (1 gallon/3.8 liter) chamber vacuum pouch and vacuum seal, or to a large zip-closure cooking pouch and use Archimedes' Principle (page 60) and seal. Submerge the pouch in the water bath until needed.

herb roasted
lamb loin

Serves 8
Cooking time: 45 minutes

1. Fill and preheat the water oven to 135°F (57°C).

2. Cut the lamb loins into 4-ounce (150 g) portions.

3. In a sauté pan over medium-high heat, sauté the portions in 1 tablespoon (15 ml) of the olive oil until golden brown on all sides.

4. Cool the lamb portions for a few minutes on a wire rack, and then put them into small (1 quart/0.9 liter) cooking pouches, fold over the open ends, secure with clips, and refrigerate.

5. On the stove in a pot of salted boiling water, blanche the fresh herbs, then plunge them into an ice water bath to arrest the cooking; wring the herbs dry, chop well, and whisk them with the remaining olive oil and dried spices.

2 pounds (32 oz/0.9 kg) lamb loin, cleaned of silver skin and fat

¼ cup (2 fl oz/60 ml) extra virgin olive oil (divided use)

3 tablespoons (45 ml) rosemary leaves

3 tablespoons (45 ml) marjoram leaves

¼ cup (0.4 oz/10g) Italian flat-leaf parsley

¼ cup (0.4 oz/10 g) fresh mint leaves

3 tablespoons (15 ml) chopped chives

1 tablespoon (15 ml) ground fennel seed

1 teaspoon (5ml) ground cumin seed

3 tablespoons (45 ml) unsalted butter

2 tablespoons (30 ml) kosher salt

1 tablespoon (15 ml) orange zest, minced

6. In another small pot over medium heat, warm the butter with the salt and orange zest.

7. Whisk the butter into the herbed olive oil, divide this mixture evenly among the cooking pouches with the lamb portions, massage to coat the meat with the oils, and vacuum seal.

8. Submerge the pouches in the water bath and cook for 25 minutes.

9. Remove the lamb from the pouches, plate, and serve.

Michael
Solomonov

Chef and Owner of Zahav in Philadelphia, Pennsylvania

53

red kuri squash poached in butter

54

lamb belly with Turkish spice

57

short ribs with Yemenite spice

59

celery salad

squash

1 (4 lb/450 g) red kuri squash, peeled, seeded, and cut into wedges or large cubes

⅓ cup (2 oz/57 g) kosher salt

¼ cup (2 oz/60 g) unrefined sugar

1 stick (4 oz/113g) unsalted butter, browned and refrigerated

2 tablespoons (30 g) white sesame seeds

Coarsely ground black pepper, to taste

Serves 4
Cooking time: 2 hours

1. In a bowl, sprinkle the squash with the salt, toss to coat, and let it sit at room temperature for 3 hours.

2. Fill and preheat the water oven to 158°F (70°C).

3. Wipe the salt from the squash and toss with the sugar.

4. Put the seasoned squash in a single layer into a large (1 gallon/3.8 liter) cooking pouch. Add the butter and vacuum seal.

5. Submerge the pouch in the water bath and cook for 2 hours.

6. When ready to serve, transfer the squash from the pouch to a serving bowl and toss with sesame seeds and black pepper.

lamb belly

with Turkish spice

Serves 4
Cooking time: 36 hours

1. Fill and preheat the water oven to 145°F (63°C).

2. In a small bowl, combine all the spices, season the lamb bellies all over with the mixture, cover, and refrigerate for 12 hours.

3. Remove the lamb bellies from the refrigerator, sprinkle one surface of each belly with the transglutaminase, and press two bellies together to form a single, thicker "lamb steak." Wrap the steak with plastic wrap and refrigerate for another hour to bond.

4. Put each plastic-wrapped steak into a small (1 quart/0.9 liter) cooking pouch and vacuum seal.

5. Submerge the pouches in the water bath and cook for 36 hours.

1 teaspoon (5 ml) ground cinnamon

1 teaspoon (5 ml) ground black pepper

1 teaspoon (5ml) ground coriander

1 teaspoon (5 ml) ground urfa (or cayenne) pepper

Kosher salt to taste

2 (8 oz/240g) lamb bellies, cut in half

1 teaspoon (5 ml) transglutaminase

Transglutaminase is a naturally occurring enzyme, often referred to as "meat glue" for its property to bind proteins together. It is sold commercially as Activa® and available through restaurant suppliers or on amazon.com.

For plating

Dressed lettuce or chopped cucumber

6. Remove the pouches and cool in an ice bath (half ice, half water) for 45 minutes to 1 hour, replenishing ice as needed. Refrigerate for up to 48 hours if not proceeding immediately.

7. When ready to finish, heat a pan or plancha to high heat, remove the lamb from the pouch, remove and discard the plastic wrap, and sear the lamb until both sides are well browned.

Chef's recommended plating

1. Slice each lamb steak into four long pieces.

2. Plate each slice with a little dressed lettuce or chopped cucumber.

short ribs

with Yemenite spice

1 tablespoon (15 ml) ground cumin

1 tablespoon (15 ml) ground turmeric

1 tablespoon (15 ml) ground black pepper

2 tablespoon (30 ml) kosher salt

4 beef short ribs, on the bone

For plating

Celery Salad (page 59)

Serves 4

Cooking time: 24½ hours

1. Fill and preheat the water oven to 145°F (63°C).

2. In a small bowl, mix together the spices and the salt and distribute evenly over the short ribs.

3. Put the ribs, two to a pouch in a single layer, into small (1 quart/0.9 liter) cooking pouches, and vacuum seal.

4. Submerge the pouches in the water bath and cook for 24 hours.

5. After cooking, remove the pouches from the water bath and allow them to sit at room temperature for 30 minutes. If not using immediately, cool in stages, submerging the pouches in cold water for an additional 30 minutes, and finally in an ice water bath for 1 hour. Refrigerate for up to 2 days.

6. When ready to finish, heat a grill or grill pan to high heat.

7. Remove the ribs from the pouches and sear the meat on the grill. Use the liquid in

the bags to baste the meat until a crust has developed and the interior of the meat is hot. Remove from the grill and allow the meat to rest for 5 minutes.

Chef's recommended plating

1. Present each rib on its own plate.

2. Garnish with Celery Salad and serve immediately.

celery salad

1 rib celery
3 dates, pitted
10 parsley leaves
½ lemon, for juice
kosher salt, to taste

Serves 4
Preparation time: 5 minutes

1. Coarsely chop the celery, dates, and parsley.

2. Add the lemon juice, and mix well.

3. Season with Kosher salt to taste.

Measurements

Because of the precisely controlled temperatures used in sous vide cooking, recipes can be reproduced perfectly time after time. But as with any culinary technique, the success of the recipe also depends on correctly measured ingredients. Different ingredients are measured in different ways and, depending on where you live, using different measuring utensils. In order to ensure that our recipes can be successfully prepared by everyone—whether you live in Des Moines or Tokyo—the ingredient amounts have been specified using both volume and mass (weight).

Mass equivalencies for US volume measuring spoons (teaspoons and tablespoons) are given as UK metric measuring spoons (milliliters). (The same size measuring spoons in Asia are specified in grams.) The volume measure conversions based on cooking utensils are: ¼ teaspoon = 1.25 ml spoon; ½ teaspoon = 2.5 ml spoon; 1 teaspoon = 5 ml spoon; 1 tablespoon = 15 ml spoon.

For liquids, a 1 cup measurement, as well as fractions of a cup, are converted to weights based on 8 fl oz being equivalent to 240 ml, the US FDA standard. Dry volume measures, as well as fluid measurements greater than 1 cup volume, have been converted to actual weights. For example, 1 cup of crumbled Feta cheese weighs 5 oz/150 g, while 1 cup of fine cornmeal weighs 6.3 oz/186 g. A pint of liquid is accurately converted to 16 fl oz/473 ml, not estimated based on 240 ml per cup. The accuracy of these conversions make it possible to successfully produce the recipes worldwide.

Archimedes' Principle

The principle, first stated by Greek mathematician and physicist Archimedes, in the second century BCE, states: Any object, wholly or partially immersed in a fluid, is buoyed up by a force equal to the weight of the fluid displaced by the object. In sous vide cooking, we can use this property to displace the air in a cooking pouch containing liquid. When we fill a pouch with food and liquid, because air is lighter than water, we can use this displacement principle to force the residual air from the pouch, and then zip it closed to create a mostly airless environment inside the pouch. Here are the simple steps:

1. Fill a zip-closure cooking pouch with food and fluid.

2. Lower the filled pouch, with the zip closure still open, into the water bath (or into a large pot of cooler water, if you prefer.)

3. The weight of the water in the bath or pot will press against the sides of the pouch and force the air out as you lower the zip closure to the surface of the water.

4. Once the zip closure is at the surface and most of the air has been evacuated from the pouch, zip it closed. The zip-sealed pouch should now stay submerged.

This principle can be used to evacuate most of the air from a cooking pouch containing liquid, which can be difficult to handle with a suction vacuum sealer. Using a zip-closure cooking pouch and Archimedes' Principle makes it easy to prepare sous vide sauces, syrups, glazes, infusions, ice cream bases, soups, stews, braises, and more.

ISBN: 978-0-9844936-8-5

Printed in the United States of America.
First Edition
1 2 3 4 5 6 7 8 9 10

Book design by Faith Keating

ParadoxPress

More Cookbooks
from Paradox Press

Easy Sous Vide

Sous Vide Meat

Sous Vide Poultry

Sous Vide One Pots

Sous Vide Barbecue

Sous Vide Holiday

Sous Vide Cocktails

Sous Vide
for the Home Cook